Horizons

Phonics and Reading

K

Book 1
Lessons 1–40

Author: Pollyann O'Brien, M.A.

Editor: Alan L. Christopherson, M.S.

Alpha Omega Publications, Inc. • Rock Rapids, IA

Horizons Phonics K, Book 1
© MM Published by Alpha Omega Publications, Inc.
804 N. 2nd Ave. E.
Rock Rapids, IA 51246-1759

Printed in the United States of America

ISBN 978-0-7403-0137-7

- - - - - - - - - - - - - -

Read the alphabet.

a b c d e f g h i j k l m

n o p q r s t u v w x y z

Look at the letter a.

It is the first letter of the alphabet. The letter a is a vowel and

can be used at the beginning, middle, or end of a word.

The vowel a makes the sound we hear at the beginning of

Andy Alligator eating an apple.

Rule 1: **Every word must have a vowel in it.**

Rule 2: **If there is only one vowel in a word, it usually**

uses the short-vowel sound.

apple

add

alligator

astronaut

anteater

1

1 Put a circle around the pictures that start with the sound of ă as in
Andy Alligator eating an apple.

2 Look at the pictures of words with the sound of short ă in the middle
of the word. Say the words.

Măx   făn   băt   măd

3 Underline the short ă in the middle of the word. Say the sound of
short ă as in Andy Alligator.

băt   dăd   păn   răn

4 **Review the alphabet.**

5 **Look at the capital A. Trace over the lines. Follow the numbers and lines to make the letter.**

6 **Look at the lowercase a. Trace over the lines. Start at the top of the curve and circle around. Lift the pencil to start the straight line down.**

7 **Put a circle around the capital A. Put an x on the lowercase a.**

A A a A a B a a A A a b a A a

a A A b A b a B A a a A A b a

8 **Practice printing the capital A and lowercase a on the lines below.**

9 **Print an a under the pictures that start with the short ă sound.**

_____   _____   _____   _____
- - - - - - - - -   - - - - - - - - -   - - - - - - - - -   - - - - - - - - -
_____   _____   _____   _____

_____   _____   _____   _____
- - - - - - - - -   - - - - - - - - -   - - - - - - - - -   - - - - - - - - -
_____   _____   _____   _____

10 **Draw a picture of an ant eating an apple. Print an a under the picture.**
Color the ant BLACK. Color the apple RED.

_____
- - - - - - - - -
_____

 4

_____

Read the alphabet.

a b c d e f g h i j k l m

n o p q r s t u v w x y z

Look at the letter b.

The letter b is a consonant and can be used at the
beginning, middle, or end of a word.

The consonant b makes the sound we hear at the
beginning of baseball and bat.

bathtub

ball

Bible

bat

bottle

bag

5

1 **Put a circle around the pictures that start with the sound of** b **as in** big boy **with a** baseball bat**.**

2 **Underline the sound** ba **you hear in the words below the pictures.**

bat   bag   band   bank

3 **Put a circle around the pictures whose words end with the** b **sound.**

bathtub   cab   horse   box

4 **Review the alphabet.**

5 **Look at the capital B. Trace over the lines. Follow the numbers and lines to make the letter.**

B B B B B B

6 **Look at the lowercase b. Trace over the lines. Follow the numbers and lines to make the letter.**

b b b b b b

7 **Put a circle around the capital B. Put an x on the lowercase b.**

B a B b B B b a b b B B A b b

A b B A B b B a b B b a b b B

8 **Practice printing the capital B and lowercase b on the lines below.**

B

b

⑨ **Print** ba **under the pictures that start with the sound of** ba **as in** bat.

⑩ **Draw a picture of Big Boy Bob playing baseball. Put a bat in Bob's hands.**
Print b **under Bob's blue bat. Put a capital** B **under Big Boy Bob.**

_____
- - - - - - - - - - - - - - - -
_____

Read the alphabet.

a b c d e f g h i j k l m

n o p q r s t u v w x y z

Look at the letter d.
The letter d is a consonant and can be used at the
beginning, middle, or end of a word. The consonant d
makes the sound we hear at the beginning of
Dandy Doll dries the dishes.

Dad

dog

Dd

desert

doll

desk

9

1 Put a circle around the pictures that start with the sound of d as in
Dandy Doll dries the dishes. Put an x on the pictures that do not
start with the sound of the letter d.

2 Circle the words under the pictures that begin with the sound of da.

| fish | dad | doctor | dam |

3 Circle the letters you hear as the beginning sound of the word.

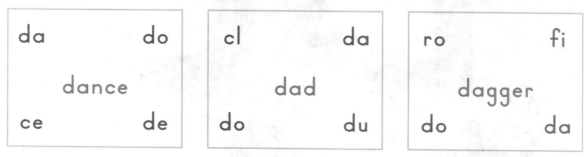

da	do	cl	da	ro	fi
dance		dad		dagger	
ce	de	do	du	do	da

4 **Review the alphabet.**

5 **Look at the capital** D. **Trace over the lines. Follow the numbers and lines to make the letter.**

D D D D D D

6 **Look at the lowercase d. Trace over the lines. Follow the numbers and lines.**

d d d d d d

7 **Put a circle around the capital** D. **Put an x on the lowercase** d.

D d a d b D c D d a d B D d b b

a d D D d b d A C D d D d b d

8 **Practice printing the capital** D **and lowercase** d **on the lines below.**

D

d

11

9 **Put a circle around the words starting with the sound of d.**
Trace and write the first letter for each picture.

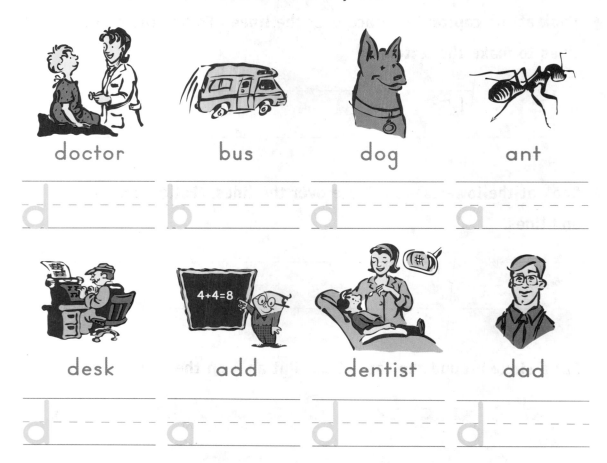

doctor   bus   dog   ant

d   b   d   a

desk   add   dentist   dad

d   a   d   d

10 **Print da under the pictures that start with the sound of da.**

11 **How many words begin with the sound of da?** _____

12 **Can you think of other words that begin with the sound of d?**

Read the alphabet.

a b c d e f g h i j k l m
n o p q r s t u v w x y z

Look at the letter o.

The letter o is a vowel and can be used at the beginning, middle, or end of a word. The vowel o makes the sound we hear at the beginning of Ollie Octopus.

Review Rule 1:   Every word must have a vowel in it.

Review Rule 2:   If there is only one vowel in a word, it usually uses the short-vowel sound.

olive

octopus

ox

ostrich

otter

13

1 **Put a circle around the pictures that start with the sound of ŏ as in** **O**llie **O**ctopus eating **o**lives.

2 **Put a circle around the words with the ŏ in the middle of the word.**

ducks   log   box   Bob

hog   doll   cob   dog

_____

3 **Review the alphabet.**

4 **Practice printing the letter o. Follow the numbers and lines to make the letter. Print a capital ○ and a lowercase o on the lines below.**

5 **Print an o under each picture that starts with the short sound of ŏ.**

6 **Circle the letters that make the sound of ŏ in each word below.**

map   log   lock   long

7 **Put a circle around each picture that has a** short ŏ **in the middle.**

8 **Practice printing the letters** ba.

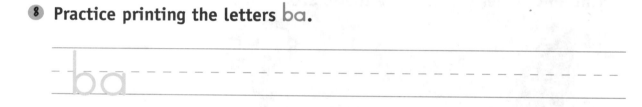

ba

9 **Practice printing the consonant before the vowel** o.

bo

do

10 **Practice printing the word** dad.

dad

Read the alphabet.

a b c d e f g h i j k l m

n o p q r s t u v w x y z

Look at the letter c.

The letter c is a consonant and can be used at the beginning, middle, or end of a word. The consonant c makes the sound we hear at the beginning of Candy Cat.

cake

cup

cat

cap

candle

candy

17

1 Put a circle around the pictures that start with the sound of c as in Candy Cat.

2 Circle the pictures that begin with the sound of ca.

3 Circle the letters that make the beginning sound you hear in each word.

do ca fi   ca qu mo   ni bo ca   la ba ca

4 Review the alphabet.

5 Practice printing the capital C and lowercase c on the lines below.

C   C   C

c   c   c

6 Put a circle around the capital C. Put an x on the lowercase c.

C B C c d c c a C C A c a c D

b c C C B c c C c c C a C A c

7 Put a circle around the letters that make the sound of ca.

c a	g a	b u	c a	c a
m a	c a	c a	g a	c a

8 Count the sets of letters making the sound of ca. _____

9 **Put a circle around the picture that starts with the given sound.**

Write the beginning sounds on the lines below the circled pictures.

Read the alphabet.

a b c d e f g h i j k l m

n o p q r s t u v w x y z

Look at the letter e.

The letter e **is a vowel and can be used at the beginning, middle, or end of a word. The vowel** e **makes the sound we hear at the beginning of** Eddie Elephant sat on the edge.

Review Rule 1: Every word must have a vowel in it.

Review Rule 2: If there is only one vowel in a word, it usually uses the short-vowel sound.

elk

engine

Ed

elbow

elephant

21

1 Put a circle around each picture that begins with the sound of e as in Eddie Elephant sat on the edge.

2 Circle the words under the pictures that have a short ĕ sound in the middle.

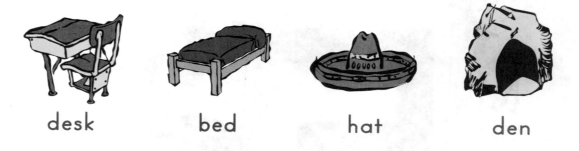

desk   bed   hat   den

3 Read the puzzle phrases.

elephant on a bed

belt on legs

④ **Put a circle around the pictures that start with the sound of** dĕ.

⑤ **Put a circle around the pictures that start with the sound of** bĕ.

Beth   doll   mad   bed

Ben   legs   belt   beg

⑥ **Draw a line to the words that are alike.**

dad	Ed
Ed	bed
elephant	elephant
bed	dad

tent	dot
Ted	cot
cot	tent
dot	Ted

7 **Review the alphabet.**

8 **Practice printing the letter e. Follow the numbers and lines to make the letter. Print a capital E and a lowercase e on the lines below.**

E   E   E

e   e   e

9 **Print an e under each picture that starts with the short vowel sound ĕ.**

_____   _____   _____   _____

10 **Put a circle around each picture that has a short ĕ sound in the middle.**

11 **Practice writing the first consonant and adding a short ĕ.**

be _____   de _____

Read the alphabet.

a b c d e f g h i j k l m

n o p q r s t u v w x y z

Look at the letter f.
The letter f is a consonant and can be used at the beginning,
middle, or at the end of a word. The consonant f makes the
sound we hear at the beginning of Freddie Fish found a fork.

fish

frog

family

fork

fan

feather

fox

1 Put a circle around the pictures that start with the sound of f as in Freddie Fish.

2 Circle the words that start with the sound of fă.

duck   fan   candle   family   fat

3 Circle the letters that make the beginning sound you hear in each word.

fox   cot   fed   fan

fo ca co   ca co to   fe de af   ca fa go

4 Put a circle around each picture that starts with the sounds of fĕ.

5 Put a circle around the letters that make the sound of fă.

fa   da   fa   ba   fa   fa

6 Read the sentences.

Bab fed a cat.   Dad fed the cat.

26

LESSON 7
Letter f

7 **Review the alphabet.**

8 **Practice printing the capital F and lowercase f on the lines below.**

9 **Put a circle around the capital F. Put an x on the lowercase f.**

F f b F d B F F f f F F c f f A

F F f f F b F d B F F f c f d F

10 **Circle the words below the pictures that start with the consonant f.**

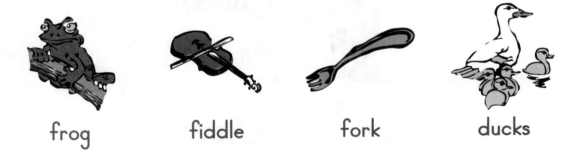

frog   fiddle   fork   ducks

11 **Write and sound out the make-up words below.**

feb   fab   fef   fof

12 **Practice printing the first consonant, followed by a vowel.**

fat   fan   fad   fender

13 **Read and trace the puzzle sentence, then write it on the lines below.**

Ed fed a bed.

Read the alphabet.

a b c d e f g h i j k l m

n o p q r s t u v w x y z

Look at the letter g.
The letter g is a consonant and can be used at the beginning,
middle, or end of a word. The consonant g makes the sound
we hear at the beginning of Gary Goat goes golfing.

gift

goat

goose

Gg

gorilla

gate

① **Put a circle around each picture that begins with the sound of g as in Gary Goat loves garbage.**

② **Put a circle around each picture that begins with the sound of the letters gă.**

③ **Put a circle around each picture that begins with the sound of the letters gŏ.**

④ **Look where the g comes in the following words. Put a circle around the g if it comes at the end of the word.**

bag   fed   gag   cog   dog   fat

⑤ **Circle the words your teacher says.**

| bed   can   cab | God   gas   bag |

⑥ **Review the alphabet.**

⑦ **Practice printing the capital G and lowercase g on the lines below.**

⑧ **Put a circle around the capital G. Put an x on the lowercase g.**

G g g G g G G B g g G g A d G

f G g g g G g G G B g g a b g

⑨ **Practice printing g under each picture that starts with the sound of g.**

⑩ **Practice writing the letter g followed by a vowel.**

⑪ **Write and sound out the make-up words.**

gac   gaf   dag   gat

⑫ **Read and trace the puzzle sentence, then write it on the lines below.**

Dad fed an egg.

Read the alphabet.

a b c d e f g h i j k l m

n o p q r s t u v w x y z

Look at the letter i.

The letter i is a vowel and can be used at the beginning, middle,

or end of a word. The vowel i makes the sound we hear

at the beginning of Iggie Inchworm itches.

Review Rule 1:   Every word must have a vowel in it.

Review Rule 2:   If there is only one vowel in a word,

it usually uses the short-vowel sound.

inchworm

ill

iguana

Ii

igloo

insect

1. Put a circle around each picture with a short ĭ sound at the beginning as in Iggie Inchworm itches.

2. Put an x on each picture with a short ĭ in the middle.

3. Circle the letter you hear that makes the beginning sound.

d f	b e	o f
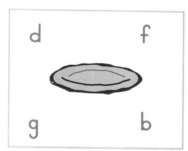		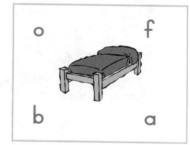
g b	d g	b a

4. Circle the letter that makes the middle vowel sound you hear.

a e	a e	a e
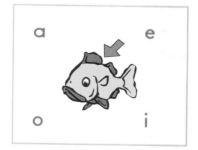		
o i	o i	o i

5 Review the alphabet.

6 Practice printing the vowel i. Follow the numbers and lines to make the letter. Print a capital I and a lowercase i on the lines below.

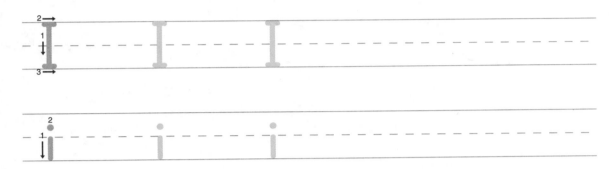

7 Print i under each picture that starts with the vowel sound i.

8 The capital I can stand alone and make a word. It has the long ī sound that you hear in the word eye. Read the phrases below and write them on the lines below.

I did

I do

9 **Practice printing and saying the sounds the letters make.**

ba	be	bi	bo

da	de	di	do

fa	fe	fi	fo

ga	ge	gi	go

10 **Read together with your teacher. Mark each short vowel with the sign that tells you the vowel is short.**

da	de	di	do	fo
fa	fe	fi	ga	go

11 **Read the words together. Mark each short vowel ă ĕ ĭ ŏ.**

Dan	God	dig	dog	fed
rib	fell	fin	bag	Bob

Read the alphabet.

a b c d e f g h i j k l m

n o p q r s t u v w x y z

Look at the letter h.

The letter h **is a consonant and usually comes at the beginning of a word. The consonant** h **makes the sound you hear at the beginning of** Happy Hippopotamus played hopscotch.

hockey

horn

hog

horse

hat

1 Put a circle around each picture that starts with the h sound.

2 Put a circle around each picture that starts with the hă sound.

3 Put a circle around each picture that starts with the hĕ sound.

4 Put a circle around each picture that starts with the hŏ sound.

5 Put a circle around each picture that starts with the hĭ sound.

  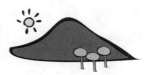

LESSON 10
Letter h

⑥ **Review the alphabet.**

⑦ **Practice printing the capital** H **and the lowercase** h **on the lines below.**

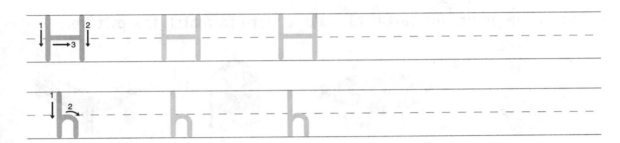

⑧ **Put a circle around the capital** H. **Put an x on the lowercase** h.

H c h h d H H g c h h e H h A H

h h o H h d H H g c h h e H h f

⑨ **Look at the pictures. Print** h **under each picture that starts with the sound of** h.

39

10 **Read the make-up words.**

h a b   h e f   h i b   h o m

11 **Put in the beginning letter to make a word to match the picture.**

___ad   ___og   ___ag   ___ed

12 **Look at the pictures. Add s at the end to show more than one thing.**

hog   bed   fan   dog

hog___   bed___   fan___   dog___

40

13 **Read the sentences. Trace, then print them on the lines below.**

The beginning of a sentence must have a capital letter.

This (.) is a period. Put a period at the end of the sentence.

Ed fed the dog.

Bob had a bed.

14 **Read each puzzle sentence and draw a line to the picture it matches.**

Bob had
a hot dog.

Dad hid a hog.

Ed fed a cab.

15 **Look at the pictures. Print the first two letters under each picture.**

cab   bad   can   dot

cob   Bob   add   cot

16 **Draw a picture of your home.**

Read the alphabet.

a b c d e f g h i j k l m

n o p q r s t u v w x y z

Look at the letter u.

The letter u is a vowel and can be used at the beginning
or middle of a word. The vowel u makes the sound we hear
at the beginning of Umpire under the umbrella.

Review Rule 1:   Every word must have a vowel in it.

Review Rule 2:   If there is only one vowel in a word,
                      it usually uses the short-vowel sound.

up

usher

umbrella

upside down

1 **Put a circle around each picture that starts with a short ŭ sound.**

2 **Put a circle around the short ŭ sound in the middle of each word.**

rŭg   pŭppy   bŭg   rŭn

3 **Put an x on each picture that begins with the sound of dŭ.**

4 **Underline each picture that begins with the sound of fŭ.**

44

⑤ **Put a circle around each picture that begins with the sound of bŭ.**

⑥ **Underline each picture that begins with the sound of cŭ.**

⑦ **Put an x on each picture that begins with the sound of gŭ.**

⑧ **Put a circle around all the words in the word bank that have the sound of short ŭ in the middle.**

 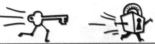

puff	rug	top	jug	cut
gull	sun	cob	run	bud
bad	nut	bed	cuff	mud

9 **Review the alphabet.**

10 **Practice printing the vowel u. Follow the numbers and lines to make the letter. Print a capital ∪ and a lowercase u on the lines below.**

11 **Print a u under the words that have a short ŭ sound.**

upside down   cut   mug   umbrella

12 **Draw a line from the picture to the word.**

dug

bag

bug

bud

46

Read the alphabet.

a b c d e f g h i j k l m

n o p q r s t u v w x y z

Look at the letter t.
The letter t is a consonant and can be used at the
beginning, middle, or end of a word. The consonant t makes the
sound we hear at the beginning of Ten tired turtles trotting.

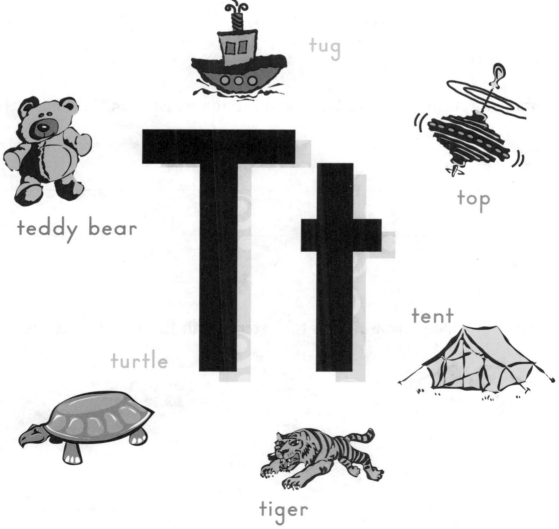

tug

teddy bear

top

T t

tent

turtle

tiger

① **Put a circle around the pictures that start with the sound of t.**

② **Put a circle around the words that end with the sound of t.**

hat	ant	cat	dad	fin
fat	hit	dot	met	led
mitt	rat	hut	bat	lid
rod	net	dig	cup	fit

③ **Review the alphabet.**

④ **Practice printing the capital T and the lowercase t on the lines below.**

⑤ **Print a t under each picture that starts with the sound of the letter t.**

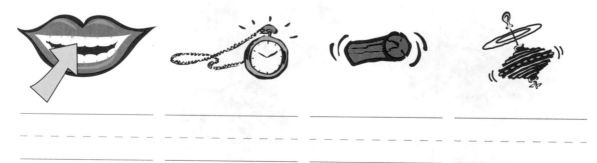

48

6 **Read the sentences. Print them on the lines below. Remember that each sentence must begin with a capital letter and end with a period.**

Tad had a hat.

Ted had a tug.

Dad had a dog.

7 **Read the make-up words.**

tup   teb   taf   tud

8 **Read the puzzle sentence and draw a line to the correct picture.**

Ben has a
dog on a tug.

Ted had a big
dot on a bed.

49

9 Practice writing the letter t with the vowel letter. Say the sound as you print the letter.

ta

te

ti

to

tu

10 Put a circle around each word that starts like the letters in the box.

ta	tab	sack	tan	tablet
te	test	telephone	ten	bed
ti	film	tip	tin	tick
to	foot	top	toss	tot
tu	tub	tug	tuff	put

Read the alphabet.

a b c d e f g h i j k l m

n o p q r s t u v w x y z

Look at the letter n.

The letter n is a consonant and can be used at the beginning, middle, or end of a word. The consonant n makes the sound we hear at the beginning of Nurse Nancy counted numbers.

neck

net

nurse

nut

Ned

nail

51

1 **Put a circle around the picture that starts with the sound of n.**

2 **Put a circle around the picture that starts with the sound of nă.**

3 **Draw a line from the word to the correct picture.**

nut

net

nap

Ned

④ **Review the alphabet.**

⑤ **Practice printing the capital** N **and lowercase** n **on the lines below.**

N   N   N

n   n   n

⑥ **Read the words that start with the consonant** n**. Then print them on the lines below.**

Ned   nap   Nan   net

⑦ **Spell the words to match the pictures.**

pan   ran   nut

53

8 Look at the words in the word bank. Print the words in the blank so the sentence is correct.

| ran | nap | fan | nut |

1. Nan had a _____ .

2. Ned had his lips on a _____ .

3. The _____ is in the den.

4. Dad _____ up a hill.

9 Practice printing the following words and phrases.

| fun | fan | nap | pan |

a bun in a bed

a hat on a hut

LESSON 13
Letter n

10 Put a circle around the picture that starts with the given sound.

Write the beginning sounds on the lines below the circled pictures.

ne

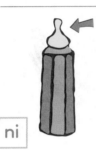   

ni

nu

no

11 **Put a circle around the picture that ends with the given sound.**

Write the ending sounds on the lines below the circled pictures.

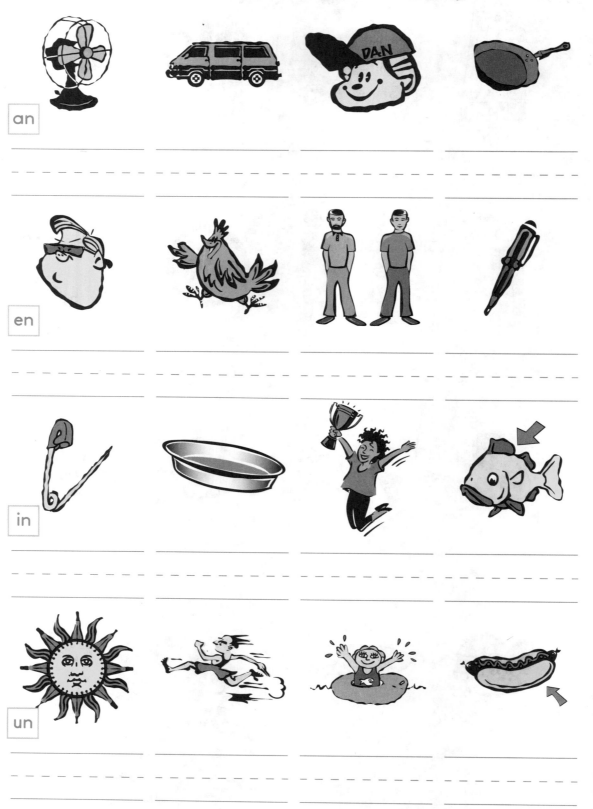

- - - - - - - - - - - -

Read the alphabet.

a b c d e f g h i j k l m

n o p q r s t u v w x y z

Look at the letter k.

The letter k is a consonant and can be used at the beginning,
middle, or end of a word. The consonant k makes the sound
we hear at the beginning of King Kangaroo has a kettle.

kite

kick

Ken

Kim

kitten

kangaroo

① **Put a circle around each picture that begins with the sound of k.**

② **Put a circle around each word that starts like the beginning letters in the box.**

ki	kit	kitten	hid	kid

ke	kettle	kite	ketchup	Ken

③ **Draw a line from the puzzle phrase to the picture it matches.**

a kitten on
a kangaroo

a kid can kick

a king on
a kettle

ketchup
on a kite

---

4 **Review the alphabet.**

5 **Practice writing the capital K and the lowercase k on the lines below.**

K   K   K

k   k

6 **Look at the pictures. Print k under each picture that starts with the sound of k.**

7 **Read the words and then print them on the lines below.**

kit   tab   Ken

8 **Read the make-up words.**

ket   kag   keb   kif

9 **Read the following sentences. Draw a line from the sentence to the picture it matches.**

Ted had the bug.

Ed can kick the can.

Ken had a cat.

The kangaroo had a king.

10 **Read the sentences. Then print them on the lines below.**

Ken had fun.

Dad fed the cub.

Ed can kick.

⑪ **Draw a line from the picture to the word.**

kid

kit

Ken

kick

kitten

⑫ **Look at the pictures. Finish spelling the words that have the letter k in them.**

___ iss ___ ite ___ ettle ___ at

___ it ___ ad ___ ing ___ im

13 **Read the sentences. Print them on the lines below. Remember to use a capital letter at the beginning and a period at the end of each sentence.**

Ed had a bug.

_____

- -

_____

Dad had a dog.

_____

- -

_____

Bob fed a dog.

_____

- -

_____

The big bug dug.

_____

- -

_____

Read the alphabet.

a b c d e f g h i j k l m

n o p q r s t u v w x y z

Look at the letter l.

The letter l is a consonant and can be used at the beginning, middle, or end of a word. The consonant l makes the sound we hear at the beginning of Lucky Leo Lion licked a lollipop.

lion

lock

lamp

lunch

lily

1 Put a circle around the pictures that start with the sound of l.

2 Put a circle around each word that starts like the beginning letters in the box.

la	ladder	map	lad	lamp
le	leg	letter	met	left
li	little	dish	list	lid
lo	lollipop	log	dog	lock
lu	buck	lump	luck	lunch

3 Put a circle around the words that have the l sound at the end of the word.

bell	sell	bent	fell	well
Jill	mill	will	Bill	hill

4 Review the alphabet.

5 Practice printing the capital L and the lowercase l on the lines below.

6 Look at the pictures. Print an l under each picture that starts with the sound of l.

7 Read the words that start with the letter l. Then print them on the lines below.

lamb

lock

little

log

8 **Look at the words in the word bank. Print the words in the blank to make a complete sentence.**

lock	lad	little

1. Ken had a _____ in his hand.

2. The _____ can kick.

3. Ed is a _____ boy.

9 **Read and then print the words below.**

log	lot	lad	left

leg	lid	lug	lob

10 **Read the make-up words.**

lub	lom	lig	lat	len	lof

- -

Read the alphabet.

a b c d e f g h i j k l m

n o p q r s t u v w x y z

Look at the letter m.

The letter m is a consonant and can be used at the beginning, middle, or end of a word. The consonant m makes the sound we hear at the beginning of Molly Monkey made music.

mask

mouse

M m

mug

monkey

muffin

67

① **Review the alphabet.**

② **Practice printing the capital M and lowercase m on the lines below.**

M   M   M

m   m   m

③ **Read the words that start with the consonant m. Then write them on the lines below.**

milk   mat   man

④ **Look at the words in the word bank. Print the words in the blank so the sentence is correct.**

mug	mat	mill

1. The _____ is on the hill.

2. Dad had a _____ in his hand.

3. The dog sat on a _____ .

LESSON 16
Letter m

5 Spell the words to match the pictures.

6 Read the funny sentences. Draw a line from the picture to the sentence it matches.

The man had a mug.

Meg had mud in the milk.

Ted had a mat on the leg.

7 **Put a circle around the picture that starts with the sound of m.**
Write the letter m under each picture that starts with m.

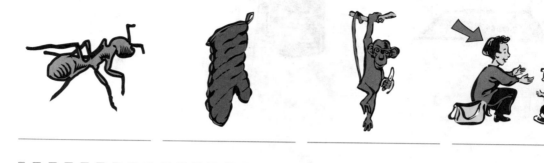

_____   _____   _____   _____

- -

_____   _____   _____   _____

8 **Read the make-up words.**

maf   meb   min   mot   mun

9 **Put a circle around the picture that starts with the given sound.**
Print the sound on the line under the circled picture.

 ma

_____   _____   _____   _____

- -

 me

_____   _____   _____   _____

- -

10 **Put a circle around the picture that starts with the given sound.**

Print the sound on the line under the circled picture.

| mi |  |  |  |  |

| mo |  |  |  |  |

| mu |  | |  |  |

11 **Practice printing the following words and phrases.**

man   ham   men   Meg

a man on a mat

a hat on a cat

12 **Read the funny sentences. Draw a line from the picture to the sentence it matches.**

A cat had a log.

The bed is on a doll.

Ed had a big hog.

Dad had a leg on a dog.

72

Read the alphabet.

a b c d e f g h i j k l m

n o p q r s t u v w x y z

Look at the letter p.

The letter p is a consonant and can be used at the beginning, middle, or end of a word. The consonant p makes the sound we hear at the beginning of Patty Pig likes to paint pictures.

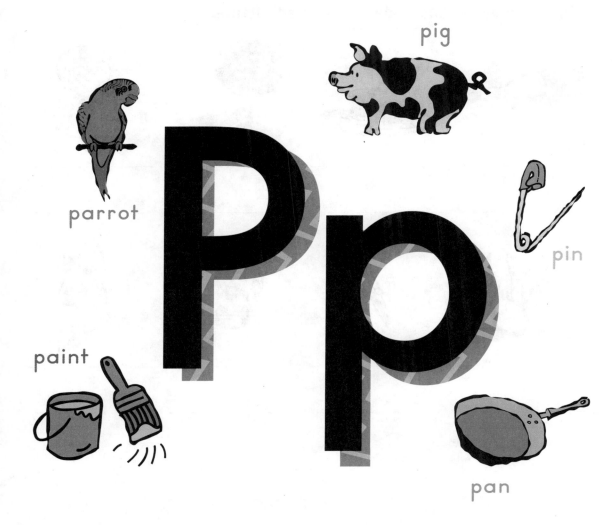

pig

parrot

pin

paint

pan

1 **Review the alphabet.**

2 **Practice printing the capital** P **and lowercase** p **on the lines below.**

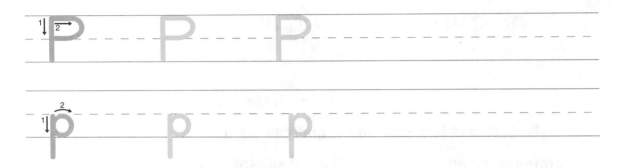

3 **Put a circle around the picture that starts with the given sound.**

Print the given sound under the circled picture.

4 **Put a circle around the picture that starts with the given sound.**

Print the given sound under the circled picture.

| pi |

| po |

| pu |

5 **Read the funny sentences. Draw a line from the picture to the sentence**

it matches.

A pad is in the mud.

A pup is in a pan.

A pin is on a pig.

75

6 **Draw a line from the word to the correct picture.**

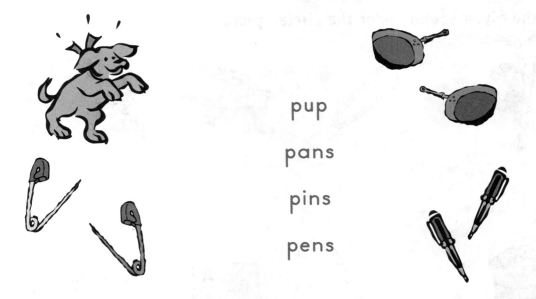

pup

pans

pins

pens

7 **Draw a line from the word to the correct picture.**

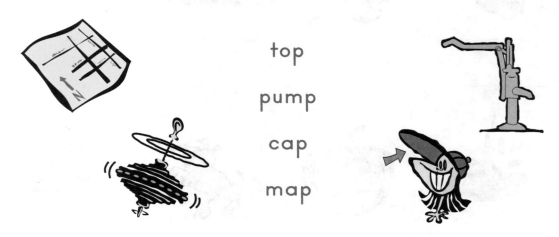

top

pump

cap

map

8 **Read the words that start with the consonant p. Then print them on the lines below.**

pig   pet   pin   pen

_____   _____   _____   _____

- - - - - -   - - - - - -   - - - - - -   - - - - - -

_____   _____   _____   _____

9 **Put a circle around the picture that starts with the sound of p.**

Print the letter under each picture that starts with the sound of p.

10 **Read the make-up words.**

pud   pom   pib   paf   ped

11 **Spell the word to match the picture.**

12 **Practice printing the following words and phrases.**

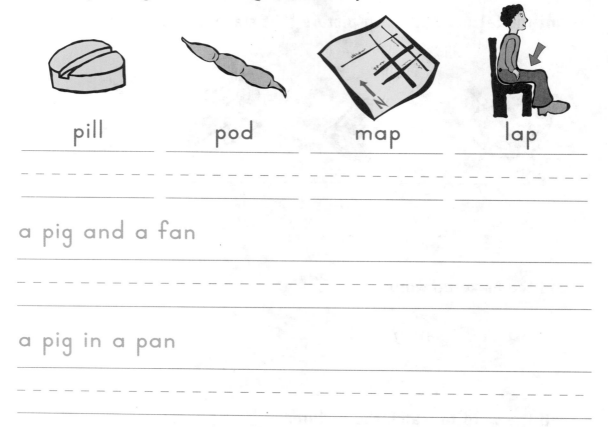

pill   pod   map   lap

a pig and a fan

a pig in a pan

13 **Look at the words in the word bank. Print the words in the blank so the sentence is correct.**

mend	pig	pan

1. The man had a _____ in the barn.

2. Mom has a _____ in her hand.

3. Peg can _____ the pants.

78

Read the alphabet.

a b c d e f g h i j k l m

n o p q r s t u v w x y z

Look at the letter r.

The letter r is a consonant and can be used at the beginning, middle, or end of a word. The consonant r makes the sound we hear at the beginning of Robby Rabbit rode a rocket.

raccoon

rocket

rake

Rr

rabbit

rooster

rat

79

① **Review the alphabet.**

② **Practice printing the capital** R **and lowercase** r **on the lines below.**

R — R — R

r — r — r

③ **Put a circle around the picture that starts with the sound of** r.

Write the letter under each picture that starts with the sound of r.

④ **Read the make-up words.**

raf   rop   rud   rin   ret

⑤ **Put a circle around the picture that starts with the given sound.**

Print the given sound under the circled picture.

ra

80

6 **Put a circle around the picture that starts with the given sound.**

Print the given sound under the circled picture.

re

ri

ro

ru

7 Draw a line from the word to the correct picture.

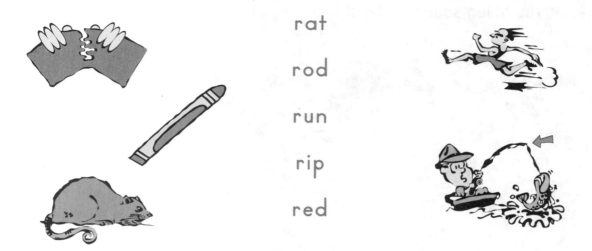

rat

rod

run

rip

red

8 Look at the words in the word bank. Print the words in the blank so the sentence is correct.

| raft | rat | run |

1. The big _____ had a hat.

2. Ed sat on a _____ .

3. Rod can _____ in the sun.

9 **Read the funny sentences. Draw a line from the picture to the sentence it matches.**

A rip is in a pan.

A rug is on a rocker.

A rag is on a rat.

10 **Read the words that start with the consonant r. Then print them on the lines below.**

rabbit   rest

_____   _____

- - - - - - - - - - - -   - - - - - - - - - - - -

rat   rub

_____   _____

- - - - - - - - - - - -   - - - - - - - - - - - -

11 **Spell the words to match the pictures.**

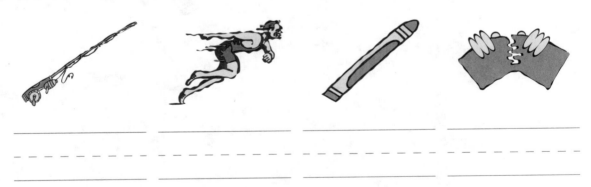

⑫ **Practice printing the following words.**

ranch   ram   ribbon

⑬ **Draw a line from the word to the picture it matches.**

raft

rap

rip

red

rod

run

Read the alphabet.

a b c d e f g h i j k l m

n o p q r s t u v w x y z

Look at the letter s.

The letter s is a consonant and can be used at the beginning, middle, or at the end of a word. The consonant s makes the soft sound we hear at the beginning of Sammy Sailor sipped soda.

sat

seal

socks

sand

sail

1 Review the alphabet.

2 Practice printing the capital S and lowercase s on the lines below.

S   S   S

s   s   s

3 Put a circle around the picture that starts with the sound of s.
Write the letter under each picture that starts with the sound of s.

_____   _____   _____   _____

4 Put a circle around the picture that starts with the given sound.

sa

se

LESSON 19
Letter s

⑤ **Put a circle around the picture that starts with the given sound.**

si

so

su

⑥ **Read the sentences. Draw a line to the picture that tells about the sentence.**

Sam sat in a tub.

Ned and Nell can sell the pans.

The big red fan is in the mud.

Bill hid in the pen.

7 **Read the words that start with the consonant s. Then print them on the lines below.**

Sam

sad

sun

sill

8 **Spell the words to match the pictures.**

sat

sip

sun

9 **Underline the pictures that end with the sound of s.**

10 **Look at the words in the word bank. Print the words in the blank so the sentence is correct.**

sing	toss	soup	sit	sand	sill

1. Meg can _____ in the sun.

2. Sip the _____ in a mug.

3. Ed can _____ a rock.

4. Jan sat on the _____ .

5. The boy played in the _____ .

6. Tom will _____ a song.

11 Practice printing the following words and phrases.

mess

miss

send

sand

sit in the sun

sit on a big hill

sit on a rug

sit on a sill

Read the alphabet.

a b c d e f g h i j k l m

n o p q r s t u v w x y z

Look at the letter q.
The letter q is a consonant and usually comes at the beginning
of a word. A q always has the letter u following it. It is
never alone. The combination of the letters qu makes the sound
we hear at the beginning of Quincy Quail under a quilt.

queen

quilt

quiver

quail

quarter

1 **Review the alphabet.**

2 **Practice printing the capital Q and lowercase q on the lines below.**

3 **Practice printing a capital Q followed by a lowercase u.**

4 **Practice printing a lowercase qu.**

5 **Practice printing a lowercase qu followed by the letter i.**

6 **Put a circle around the picture that starts with the sound of qu.**

Write the letters qu under each picture that starts with that sound.

7 **Underline the qu in each word that begins with the sound qu.**

quilt   quiver   quit   quiet   quiz

8 **Draw a line from the picture to the correct word.**

quill

quiet

queen

quail

quilt

9 **Read the following sentences. Print them on the lines below the sentence.**

1. The queen is quiet.

2. The mom and dad quail had little quails.

3. The little tot sat on a quilt.

4. Nan had to quit the run.

- -

Read the alphabet.

a b c d e f g h i j k l m

n o p q r s t u v w x y z

Look at the letter j.
The letter j is a consonant and usually comes at the beginning
of a word. The consonant j makes the sound we hear at the
beginning of Jumping Jack-in-the-box.

juice

jet

jam

jacket

jack-in-the-box

95

① **Review the alphabet.**

② **Practice printing the capital** J **and lowercase** j **on the lines below.**

J   J   J

j   j   j

③ **Put a circle around the picture that starts with the sound of** j.
Write the letter under each picture that starts with the sound of j.

④ **Read the words that start with the consonant** j. **Then print them on the lines below.**

Jill   jig   job

5 **Draw a line from the picture to the word it matches.**

jelly

job

jack-in-the-box

jacket

jump

6 **Look at the words in the word bank. Print the words in the blank so the sentence is correct.**

job	Jack	jog

1. _____ can run a lot.

2. Can Jon _____ to the pond?

3. Did Meg get a _____ ?

7 **Read the sentences. Draw a line to the picture that tells about the sentence.**

The jug is in the mud.

Jim had a big job.

Jill sat on a cot.

Jack can jig.

8 **Put a circle around the picture that starts with the given sound. Print the given sound under the circled picture.**

ja

_____

je

_____

9 **Put a circle around the picture that starts with the given sound.**

Print the given sound under the circled picture.

ji

jo

ju

10 **Spell the words to match the pictures.**

11 **Practice printing the following words and phrases.**

jet   job   Jack

a jug in the mud

a bell on a jet

Read the alphabet.

a b c d e f g h i j k l m

n o p q r s t u v w x y z

Look at the letter v.
The letter v is a consonant and usually comes at the
beginning of a word. The consonant v makes the sound
we hear at the beginning of Victor Vulture plays a violin.

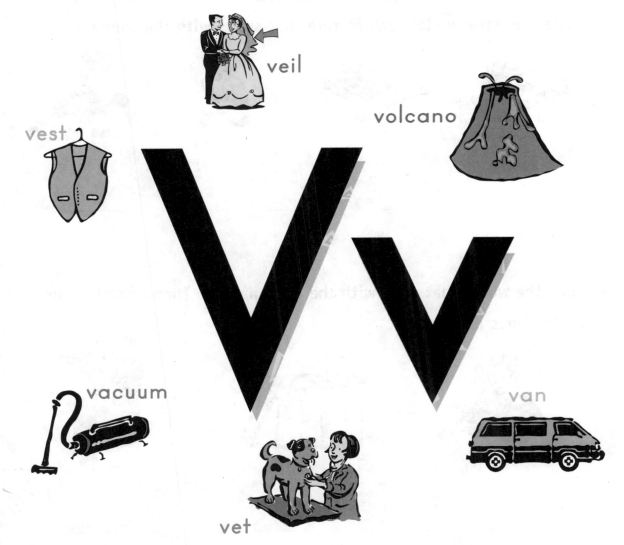

veil

volcano

vest

vacuum

van

vet

1 Review the alphabet.

2 Practice printing the capital ∨ and lowercase v on the lines below.

3 Put a circle around the picture that starts with the sound of v.

Write the letter under each picture that starts with the sound of v.

4 Read the words that start with the consonant v. Then print the words on the lines below.

violin

vat

veil

⑤ **Spell the word to match the pictures.**

⑥ **Draw a line from the picture to the word it matches.**

   vet

van

vest

          tub

⑦ **Read the sentences. Draw a line to the picture that tells about the sentence. Underline the words that begin with the letter** v.

The vet had
a cat.

The man had
a red vest.

Dad has a
tan van.

Jim has a
vine.

8 **Put a circle around the picture that starts with the given sound.**
Print the given sound under the circled picture.

9 **Look at the words in the word bank. Print the words in the blank so the sentence is correct.**

violin	vet	vest

1. The _____ had a pet dog.

2. Meg has a _____ lesson.

3. Jon has a red _____ .

10 **Practice printing the following phrases.**

a vet can pet

_____

a van in the sand

_____

the best vest

_____

11 Practice printing the following words.

quit   hip   quilt

_____   _____   _____

- - - - - - - - - -   - - - - - - - - - -   - - - - - - - - - -

_____   _____   _____

quill   quest   pill

_____   _____   _____

- - - - - - - - - -   - - - - - - - - - -   - - - - - - - - - -

_____   _____   _____

pat   quiet   quack

_____   _____   _____

- - - - - - - - - -   - - - - - - - - - -   - - - - - - - - - -

_____   _____   _____

12 Spell the word from the word bank to match the picture.

| quick | quill | cap | pup | quack | quilt |

106

Read the alphabet.

a b c d e f g h i j k l m

n o p q r s t u v w x y z

Look at the letter w.

The letter w is a consonant. When the consonant w comes at the beginning of a word, it makes the sound we hear at the beginning of Willy Wigwam wakes up.

watch

wagon

wigwam

web

waffle

watermelon

1 Review the alphabet.

2 Practice printing the capital W and lowercase w on the lines below.

3 Put a circle around the picture that has the sound of w at the beginning. Write the letter w under each word that has the w sound.

watch	worm	wig	waffle

wishbone	wall	wink	windmill

----

4 **Read the make-up words.**

wib   wem   wum   wid

5 **Read the sentences. Draw a line to the picture that tells about the sentence.**

Mom fed us a watermelon.

Jan has a red wig.

The window is up.

Jim sat in a wigwam.

6 **Read the funny question sentences. Draw a line from the picture to the sentence it matches.**

Is the walrus in the water?

Is a worm big and fat?

Can a windmill jog?

Did Don win a waffle?

7 Draw a line from the picture to the word it matches.

web

walrus

window

watermelon

wishbone

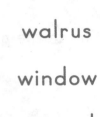

8 Read the words that start with the consonant w. Then print the words on the lines below.

woman

wag

well

web

110

9 **Look at the words in the word bank. Print the words in the blank so the sentence is correct.**

| walrus | watermelon | wig | wigwam |

1. The _____ is on a hill.

2. Dad had a red _____ .

3. The _____ sat in the sand.

4. Will you get a red _____ ?

10 **Spell the words to match the pictures.**

_____   _____   _____

⑪ **Print the following sentences. Be sure to use a capital letter on the first word of the sentence and a period or question mark at the end.**

1. The pup can wag.

2. Jill has a wig.

3. Can you jog with Will and Sam?

4. Is it red wax?

Read the alphabet.

a b c d e f g h i j k l m

n o p q r s t u v w x y z

Look at the letter y.
The letter y is a consonant. When a y comes at the
beginning of a word it makes the sound
we hear at the beginning of yellow yo-yo.

yellow

yawn

year

yell

yak

yo-yo

1 Review the alphabet.

2 Practice printing the capital Y and lowercase y on the lines below.

3 Read the words that start with the consonant y. Print the words on the lines below.

yak   yes   yellow

yard   yarn   yell

4 Read the funny question sentences. Draw a line from the picture to the sentence it matches.

Can a yak yell?

Is a cat yellow?

Can you nod for yes?

Is it a fat yardstick?

114

⑤ **Put a circle around the picture that has the sound of y at the beginning. Write the letter y under each picture that starts with the sound of y.**

⑥ **Draw a line from the picture to the word it matches.**

yardstick

yellow

yams

year

yarn

⑦ **Read the sentences below. Draw a line from the picture to the sentence it matches.**

Mom has yarn to fix a cap.

A yak is in the pen.

Jan fed us yams.

Jon has a yellow yo-yo.

8 Look at the words in the word bank. Print the words in the blank so the sentence is correct.

yarn	yellow	yak	yes

1. Can you buy a _____ yo-yo?

2. Dan had a cap of _____ .

3. The _____ is very big.

4. Jim can nod _____ . Can you?

9 Spell the words to match the pictures.

_____ _____ _____ _____

10 Read the make-up words.

yad   yub   yef   yog

Read the alphabet.

a b c d e f g h i j k l m

n o p q r s t u v w x y z

Look at the letter z.

The letter z is a consonant and can come at the beginning, middle, or end of a word. The consonant z makes the sound we hear at the beginning of the Zany Zebra lives in the zoo.

zebra

zoo

zero

zipper

zither

zeppelin

1 **Review the alphabet.**

2 **Practice printing the capital Z and lowercase z on the lines below.**

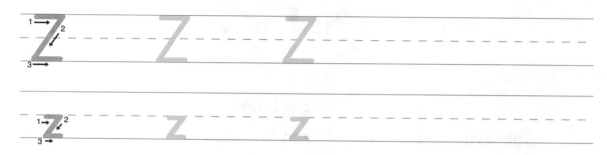

3 **Put a circle around the picture that has the sound of z at the beginning.**
Write the letter z under each word that has the z sound.

4 **Draw a line from the picture to the word it matches.**

zipper

puzzle

zebra

buzz

zither

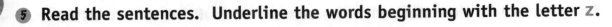

5 **Read the sentences. Underline the words beginning with the letter z.**

1. Dan went to the zoo.

2. The zipper is bad.

3. The zebra had a pen at the zoo.

4. Tom has a zither.

6 **Read the make-up words.**

zim   zot   zig   zun   zeb

7 **Read the funny question sentences. Draw a line from the picture to the sentence it matches.**

1. Can a zebra yawn?

2. Is a zipper yellow?

3. Can a zither run?

4. Is the zoo big or little?

8 **Circle the words that end in z.**

buzz   fuzz   mat   fizz   mess   fez

9 **Read the words that start with the consonant z. Print the words on the lines below.**

zoo

zither

zipper

zebra

zoom

zero

zeppelin

zucchini

zigzag

120

10 **Look at the words in the word bank. Print the words in the blank so the sentence is correct.**

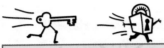

zebra	zoo	zero	zip

1. Jeb went to the _____ .

2. The _____ is not hot.

3. Can you _____ the zipper?

4. This is a _____ .

121

11 **Practice printing the following phrases.**

a little yard for the tot

a big yak

yellow yarn

a red yo-yo

a zebra at the zoo

zip or a zero

a big zipper

Read the alphabet.

a b c d e f g h i j k l m

n o p q r s t u v w x y z

Look at the letter x.
The letter x is a consonant and usually comes at the end
of a word. The consonant x makes the soft sound we hear
at the end of the words Max Fox sat on a box,
or at the beginning of the word x-ray.

box

fox

six

mix

ox

123

① Review the alphabet.

② Practice printing the capital X and lowercase x on the lines below.

③ Put a circle around the picture that has the sound of x at the end.
Write the letter x under the pictures that have the x sound.

④ Read the make-up words.

nax   dix   wox   jux

5 **Read the sentences. Underline the words ending in the letter x.**

Draw a line to the picture that tells about the sentence.

Dad can wax
the van.

Can Mom
fix the fan?

Max will get
six hens.

The fox is
in the den.

6 **Read the funny question sentences. Draw a line from the picture to**

the sentence it matches.

1. Can an ox box?

2. Can Jack sit on a fox?

3. Is Max in wax?

4. Can a fox mix?

7 **Draw a line from the picture to the word it matches.**

fox

Max

fix

box

ax

six

mix

8 **Read the words that end with the consonant x. Then print the words on the lines below.**

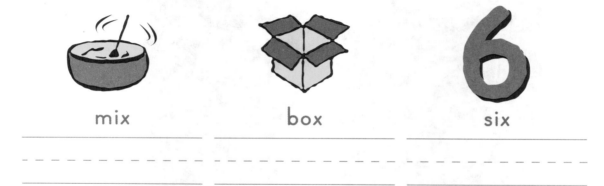

mix   box   six

_____   _____   _____

- - - - - -   - - - - - -   - - - - - -

_____   _____   _____

9 **Look at the words in the word bank. Print the words in the blank so the sentence is correct.**

| fix | fox | mix | six |

1. Mom has a pan to _____ the milk.

2. Max has _____ pet cats.

3. Can Dad _____ the mop?

4. The _____ sat on the hill.

10 **Spell the words to match the pictures.**

_____   _____   _____

_____   _____   _____

⑪ **Practice printing the following phrases.**

fix the sox

sit on a box

an ax can hit

a fox in a fix

Max Fox sat on a box

fix the x-ray

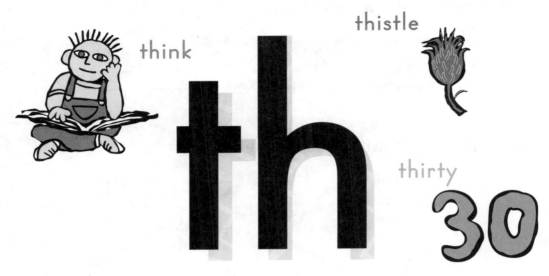

think   thistle   thirty

Definition: A consonant digraph is two consonants that stay together to make their special sound.

Look at the consonant digraph th. To make that sound, put your tongue between your teeth and say the word thin. The th sound can be used at the beginning of a word as in thin, in the middle as in wither, or at the end of a word as in path.

1 Look at the pictures and the words. Put a circle around the pictures that start with the sound of th.

thermometer   thermos   thumb   kite

thank   top   thimble   thin

129

② Practice printing **Th** with a capital **T**.

③ Practice printing **th** with lowercase letters.

④ Read the words below that start with **th**. Put a line under the **th** in each word.

the	this	them	that
then	than	thin	thug

⑤ Read the sentences. Put a line under the **th** in each word.

1. This fish is thin.
2. The thumb is fat.
3. That game is fun.
4. Thad can hop. Then he can run.

⑥ Read the make-up words.

thub   tham   thos   theg

7 **Read each word and then write it on the lines below each picture.**

thumb

thimble

thirty

thin

thank

thick

8 **Draw a line from the puzzle phrase to the picture it matches.**

a thick bug

a thin thimble

a thumb
on a rat

I thank God

9 **Find pictures that rhyme with the following words.**

thin

that

then

than

thank

10 **Write the sentence.**

I give thanks every day.

path

math

The sound of th is used at the **end** of the word as in p**a**th.

① **Put a circle around the th in the words below each picture.**

tooth	bath	moth
tenth	Beth	cloth

2 **Look at the pictures below. Circle the th to show whether the th is at the beginning or the end of the word.**

th   th   th   th   th   th   th   th

th   th   th   th   th   th   th   th

3 **Read the sentences. Draw a line from the picture to the sentence it matches.**

The lad can
do his math.

I had a bath
in a big tub.

The moth is red.

Beth can run
on a path.

Thad is the
tenth man.

4 **Read the sentences and then print them on the lines below.**

Be sure you use a capital letter for the first word in each sentence and a period at the end.

This is the thumb on the hand.

The man had a gold tooth.

5 **Spell the words below the pictures by printing the beginning sounds.**

ath   ixth   oth   ath

6 **Read the make-up words.**

dath   buth   poth   foth   nith

7 **Draw a line from the puzzle phrase to the picture it matches.**

a pig with
a math book

a moth on a dog

a path that
led to a hat

a fat cat with
a thin dog

8 **Find pictures that rhyme with the following words.**

math

dump

pick

136

‾ ‾ ‾ ‾ ‾ ‾ ‾ ‾ ‾ ‾ ‾ ‾

9 **Fill in the missing vowel in the crossword puzzle.**

Across:

A place to walk.

Down:

Water to get you clean.

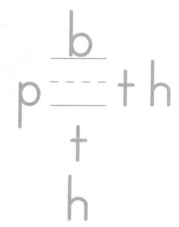

10 **Write the sentence below. Be sure to use a capital letter to start the sentence and a period at the end.**

you can do the math

-- -- -- -- -- -- -- -- -- -- -- -- -- -- -- -- -- --

-- -- -- -- -- -- -- -- -- -- -- -- -- -- -- -- -- --

11 **Read the sentence.**

The path has rocks on it.

137

LESSON 28
Consonant Digraph th

12 **Spell the words below the pictures by writing the beginning sounds.**

in   in   in

ank   ank   ank

13 **Draw a line from the puzzle phrase to the picture it matches.**

a thimble
in a bath

a path with
a big bus

138

chick

chair

cheese

chicken

Look at the consonant digraph ch.

The consonant digraph ch is usually used at the beginning or end of a word. The ch makes the sound we hear at the beginning of the word chicken. It can be used at the end of words, as in much and such.

1 Look at the consonant digraph ch. Put a circle around the pictures that start with the sound of ch.

chicken   check   chin   clock

cherry   chips   chocolate   cheese

① **Practice printing** Ch **using a capital** C**.**

Ch

③ **Practice printing** ch **using the lowercase** c**.**

ch

Rule: A person's name always starts with a capital letter, as in the name Chad. These words are called proper nouns.

④ **Read the words below that start with** ch**. Put a circle around** ch **if there is a capital** C **for a name. Put one line under** ch **if it is a lowercase** c**.**

church	Charlie	chick	champ
chin	Chad	chest	Chuck

⑤ **Read the make-up words.**

chid   dach   chep   chus   chob

6 **Read the sentences. Put a circle around each** proper noun.
Count the number of proper nouns **you can find in all the sentences.**

1. Chad went to the church with Ben.

2. I can put my hand on my chin.

3. Did Chuck see the chimp?

4. Can Charlie pick up the chick?

How many proper nouns did you find? _____

7 **Draw a line from the word to the picture it matches.**

chimp

Chad

chick

chin

check

chest

8 **Draw a line from the puzzle phrase to the picture it matches.**

a chimp in a bed

Chad on a cat

cheese in a tub

a chick on a chest

9 **Write the sentences.**

The chicken is in the pen.

I had much for God.

10 **Spell the words below the pictures by printing the beginning sounds.**

___in ___erry ___in ___ip

wheel

wheat

wheelbarrow

wheelchair

whistle

Look at the consonant digraph wh.

The consonant digraph wh is used at the beginning of a word.

The wh makes the sound we hear at the beginning of whale.

1 Put a circle around the pictures that start with the sound of wh.

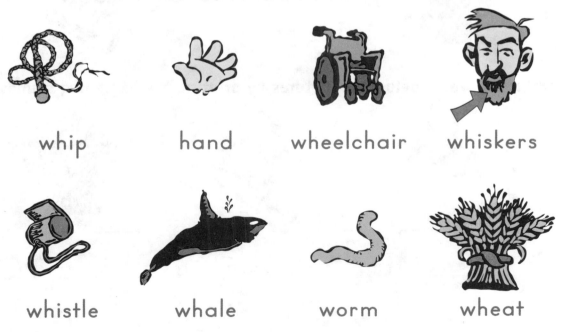

whip   hand   wheelchair   whiskers

whistle   whale   worm   wheat

143

② Practice printing Wh with a capital W.

Wh

③ Practice printing wh with a lowercase w.

wh

④ Draw a line from the word to the picture it matches.

whistle

wheel

wheat

wheelbarrow

⑤ Print the words below the pictures by printing the beginning sounds.

_____ale   _____iskers   _____eat

144

6 **Look at the pictures below. Circle the pictures that start with the sound of wh.**

7 **Learn the question words.**

Who, What, Where, When, **and** Why

8 **Underline the wh in each sentence. Draw a line to the question sentence it matches.**

Who	did the cat rest?
Where	will Dad do next?
What	has the whip?
When	did you fall down?
Why	can we go to camp?

9 **Trace the questions below, then print your name and address.**
Underline the word What**, put a circle around the word** Where**.**

What is my name?

My name is

Where do I live?

I live at

10 **Read the make-up words.**

whan   whid   whem   whos   whuf

11 **Use a** wh **beginning to make your own make-up words.**

146

LESSON 31
Review: th, ch, wh

1 **Put a circle around the pictures that start with the sound of wh.**

2 **Put an x on the pictures that start with the sound of th.**

③ **Put a square around the pictures that start with the sound of ch.**

④ **Read the make-up words.**

chom   thaf   whid   chan   thub

⑤ **Look at the pictures below. Circle the consonant digraph that the pictures start with.**

ch th wh   ch th wh   ch th wh   ch th wh

ch th wh   ch th wh   ch th wh   ch th wh

_____

- - - - - - - - - - - - - - - -

_____

6 **Draw a line from the word to the picture it matches.**

child

thumb

whistle

whale

chair

thistle

thimble

7 **Circle the word your teacher reads. Print the words you circled on the lines below.**

whip	when	whim

chap	that	this

- - - - - - - - - - - - - - - -

- - - - - - - - - - - - - - - -

thin	chin	when

chip	with	chop

- - - - - - - - - - - - - - - -

- - - - - - - - - - - - - - - -

8 **Draw a line from the picture to the puzzle phrase it matches.**

a whale in a
wheelbarrow

whiskers on
a chicken

a thimble on
a thistle

9 **Read the sentences. Underline the words that start with the sound ch. Put a circle around the words that start with the sound th. Put a box around the words that start with the sound wh.**

1. Jan is not thin.

2. Thank you, God.

3. Chad had a big chin.

4. When can Sam get wheels?

5. Tom can chop a log.

6. Who has the whistle?

shadow

shovel

sheet

sh

sheep

shave

Look at the consonant digraph sh.

The consonant digraph sh is used at the beginning or at the end of a word. The sh makes the sound we hear at the beginning of ship.

1 Put a circle around the pictures that start with the sound of sh.

ship	shelf	shirt	milk
sheep	chin	shoe	shovel

2 Practice printing sh with a capital S.

Sh

3 Practice printing sh with a lowercase s.

sh

4 Look at the pictures below. Put a circle around the pictures that start with the sound of sh.

5 Draw lines from the word to the pictures that rhyme.

lip

bath

6 **Draw a line from the word to the picture it matches.**

sheep

what

shoe

wheel

ship

shave

7 **Find these words in the word search. Circle the words.**

Across: shell, shot   **Down:** shed, ship

B C S H O T
N D H B M U
S H E L L Z
H F D P J K
I W B C E S
P T Q V P H
K Y L R N X

8 **Read the make-up words.**

shom   shen   shab   shig   shuf

153

9 Read the sentences. Print them on the lines below. Be sure you use a capital letter for the first word in each sentence and a period at the end. Underline the words that start with the sh sound.

Sam has a big ship.

_____

_____

Beth can get a shell.

_____

_____

10 Draw a line from the puzzle phrase to the picture it matches.

a doll with
a shovel

a shark in a tub

shave a pig

a shoe on
a shark

11 Spell the words below the pictures.

_____   _____   _____   _____

154

fish

sh

wish

Look at the consonant digraph sh.
The consonant digraph sh is used both at the beginning
or at the end of a word. The sh makes the sound we hear
at the end of the word fish.

① **Put a circle around the pictures that have the sound of sh at the end.**

fish   bush   kiss   radish

dish   dash   mash   cash

155

② **Practice printing** Sh **with a capital** S.

Sh

③ **Practice printing** sh **with lowercase letters.**

sh

④ **Look at the pictures below. Circle the** sh **to show whether the** sh **is at the beginning or at the end of the word.**

sh   sh   sh   sh   sh   sh   sh   sh

sh   sh   sh   sh   sh   sh   sh   sh

⑤ **Read the make-up words.**

fash   dosh   mish   besh   dush

LESSON 33
Consonant Digraph sh

6 Read the sentences. Draw a line from the picture to the sentence it matches. Underline the words that **end** with sh.

I wish I had a check.

Can you push

the dish back?

Did Jan hush?

Dan fed mush to his cat.

7 Print the words from the word bank below the word that rhymes.

lash	mash	fish	dish

hash   wish

8 **Print the sentences. Put a circle around the words that have sh at the end of the word.**

The dish is with a cup.

Is the shed red?

Ned fed mush to his dog.

Tom had to rush to see Ted.

9 **Draw a line from the puzzle phrase to the picture it matches.**

a dish on a dog

a fish in a cup

mash a ship

a bush in a net

10 **Learn to alphabetize by knowing where the letters in the alphabet come. Look at the first letter of each word. Put the words starting with** a **first. The words starting with** b **would come next because** b **is the second letter in the alphabet.**

Read these words:

    cot   dad   bat   ant

Follow the alphabet to put the words in alphabetical order.

Examples: (a) ant   (b) bat   (c) cot   (d) dad

Now print these words in alphabetical order.

    dog   ant   baby   cat

    a   b   c   d

11 **Print each row of words in alphabetical order.**

fan	elf	hog	gate
e	f	g	h

jug	log	kit	igloo
i	j	k	l

ox	pig	man	net
m	n	o	p

sit	ten	rat	quit
q	r	s	t

web	up	x-ray	vest
u	v	w	x

_____
- - - - - - - - - - - - -
_____

① **Put a circle around each picture that starts with the sound of th.**

② **Put a circle around each picture that starts with the sound of ch.**

③ **Put a circle around each picture that starts with the sound of wh.**

④ **Put a circle around each picture that starts with the sound of sh.**

⑤ Print the words from the word bank that end with sh and th.

Put a circle around the ending sound sh and th.

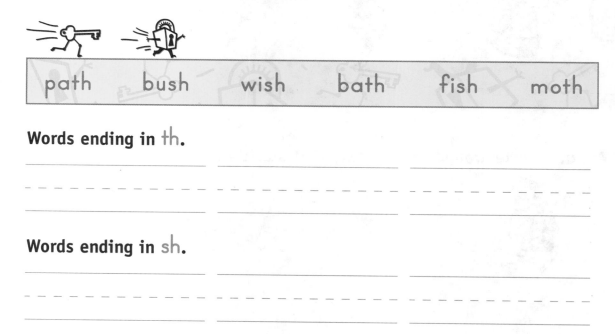

path   bush   wish   bath   fish   moth

Words ending in th.

_____   _____   _____

_____   _____   _____

Words ending in sh.

_____   _____   _____

_____   _____   _____

⑥ Draw a line from the word to the picture it matches.

shark

thumb

chick

dish

bath

⑦ Read the make-up words.

shup   chid   whaf   theg

162

8 **Circle the word your teacher reads. Print the words you circled on the lines below.**

fish	fin	ship

thin	math	chip

check	chip	when

whisper	shed	whip

9 **Draw a line from the puzzle phrase to the picture it matches.**

a fish in a bush

a check on a chick

a thin shark

a whale on the wharf

163

10 Spell the words below the pictures by printing the beginning sounds.

___icken ___ale ___imble

11 Spell the words below the pictures by printing the ending sounds.

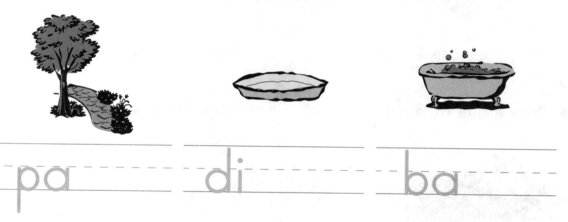

pa___ di___ ba___

12 Write the sentence below. Be sure to use a capital letter to start the sentence and a period at the end.

I wish I had a ship.

safe

cake

Silent e **Rule:**   When a word has (1) a vowel, (2) a consonant, and
(3) an e at the end, the first vowel sound is long and
the e is silent, as in cākȩ, bīkȩ, bōnȩ and tūbȩ.

1 **Look at the pictures below. Put a circle around those that have the**
long ā **sound, as in** cākȩ.

game   vase   cat   wave

cane   rake   cake   pan

② On the lines below, write the words that match the pictures.
Cross out the silent /e/ and put a straight line over the vowel ā to show
it has the long ā sound.

| cake | game | wave | rake |

_____ _____ _____ _____

- -

_____ _____ _____ _____

③ Print the words with short ă, and then add a silent /e/. Use your
markings to cross out the silent /e/ and make a straight line over the
long vowel ā.

mat   rat   tap

_____ _____ _____

- -

_____ _____ _____

cap   Jan   pal

_____ _____ _____

- -

_____ _____ _____

④ Read the words with the silent /e/ that you have printed above.

166

⑤ **Read the words with** short ă**. Mark the** short ă **vowels.**
Print the words with the short vowel.

can   mad   man

⑥ **Now look at the words which have had** silent ę̸ **added to the end of**
each word. This makes the vowel sound long **or say its own name.**
Look at the pictures and read the words below that have a long ā
sound.

cane   made   mane

⑦ **Spell the words under the pictures.**

8 **Read the sentences. Draw a line to match the picture.**

Jane ate
a big cake.

Dave sat
on a gate.

Dad will take
me to the lake.

Jan put a dime
in the safe.

9 **Circle the letters that make the ending sounds you hear.**

ābȩ ākȩ ādȩ

ābȩ ākȩ ādȩ

ābȩ ākȩ ādȩ

ākȩ ālȩ ātȩ

ākȩ ālȩ ātȩ

ākȩ ālȩ ātȩ

10 **Read the make-up words.**

dabe   cade   fape   gake   tane

11 **Draw a line from the puzzle phrase to the picture it matches.**

tape on
a rat

a baby with
a cane

a cape on
a can

a rake on
a dish

12 **Finish each sentence with a word from the word bank.**

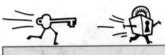

wave	lake	cake

1. I ate a _____ .

2. I can _____ my hand.

3. The _____ is big.

⑬ **Put a circle around each picture that ends with the sound of ākȼ.**

⑭ **Put a circle around each picture that ends with the sound of ālȼ.**

black

blew

The consonant blend bl is used at the beginning of a word.

The bl makes the sound we hear at the beginning of black.

1 Put a circle around the pictures that start with the sound of bl.

block

blast

sheet

sheep

blimp

blender

blade

Blake

② **Practice printing** Bl **with a capital** B.

Bl

③ **Practice printing** bl **with lowercase letters.**

bl

④ **Look at the pictures below. Print the word below the picture if it begins with the** bl **sound.**

---

5 Read the sentences. Draw a line from the picture to the sentence it matches.

Blake can blink and wink.

Sam has a black block.

Did you see the blast?

Can you blot the spot?

6 Spell the words below the pictures by printing the beginning sounds.

ender

aze

ock

ake

ake

ack

7 Draw a line from the word to the picture it matches.

blink

bluff

blimp

block

8 Read the make-up words.

blad   blef   blig   blom

9 Draw a line from the puzzle phrase to the picture it matches.

a blimp in a blender

a block on a pig

a blade with an ant

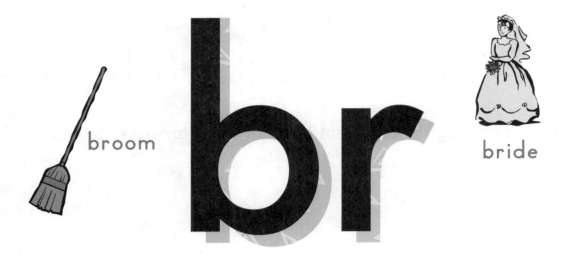

broom

br

bride

The consonant blend br is used at the beginning of a word.

The br makes the sound we hear at the beginning of brake.

1 **Put a circle around the pictures that start with the sound of br.**

brick   bridge   branch   shed

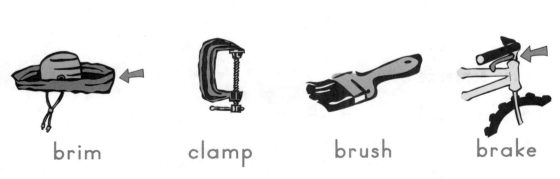

brim   clamp   brush   brake

② **Practice printing the consonant blend Br using capital B.**

Br

③ **Practice printing the consonant blend br using lowercase letters.**

br

④ **Read the words. If they have a long vowel sound, cross out the silent e and put a straight line over the vowel.**

brake   broke   blast   brave   brand

⑤ **Look at the pictures below. Print br below the picture if it begins with the br sound.**

_____   _____   _____

⑥ **Print the sentence.**

Brad had a little brush.

7 **Read the sentences. Draw a line from the picture to the sentence it matches.**

Brad broke
the vase.

Tom is
brave.

Blake has
a brush.

The brick
is red.

8 **Draw a line from the puzzle sentence to the picture it matches.**

Dan's cat sits
on a brush.

Mom's cup
is black.

Brad's pen
is on his lips.

Chad's leg is on
a big branch.

9 **Read the make-up words.**

bram   bref   brib   brun

177

10 **Spell the words under the pictures.**

_____ick   _____ush   _____ock

11 **Finish the sentences below with a word from the word bank.**

| brush | bride | block | brick |

1. Tom had the _____

   in his hand.

2. Sam can _____

   the dog.

3. The _____

   was on the bed.

4. The _____

   ran to the path.

178

clam

clown

The consonant blend cl is used at the beginning of a word.
The cl makes the sound we hear at the beginning of clock.

1 Put a circle around the pictures that start with the sound of cl.

clock   candle   clown   ship

clip   cloth   clamp   camp

② Practice printing Cl with a capital C.

Cl

③ Practice printing cl with lowercase letters.

cl

④ **Look at the pictures below. Print the beginning sound below the picture if it begins with the cl sound.**

ock   ake   ap

ub   iff   own

⑤ **Read the make-up words.**

clup   clis   clof   clen   clid

6 **Circle the letters that make the beginning sound you hear.**

bl cl br

bl cl br

bl cl br

bl cl br

bl cl br

bl cl br

bl cl br

bl cl br

th sh ch

th sh ch

th sh ch

th sh ch

th sh ch

th sh ch

th sh ch

th sh ch

7 **Print the beginning consonant blends for each word below the picture.**

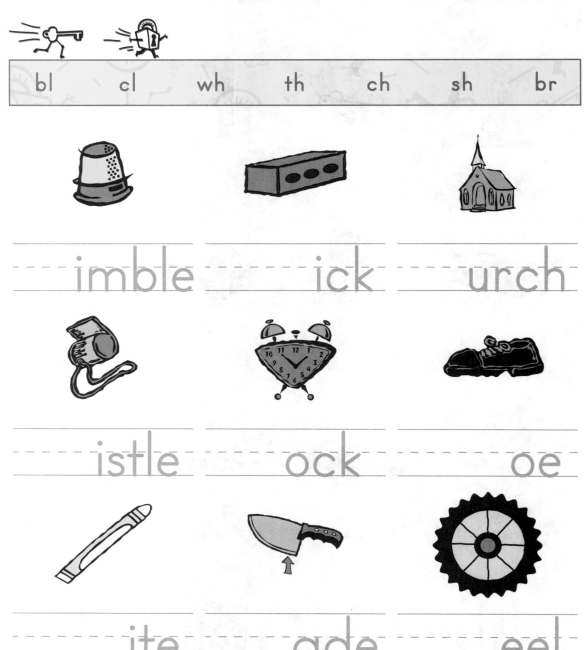

| bl | cl | wh | th | ch | sh | br |

imble   ick   urch

istle   ock   oe

ite   ade   eel

8 **Draw a line from the picture to the word it matches.**

clip

clam

cloth

clock

clamp

9 **Write the sentence below.**

Sam can clap for Chad.

10 **Spell the words under the pictures.**

block
_____

black
_____

blast
_____

blink
_____

blade
_____

Blake
_____

11 **Circle the letters that make the beginning sounds you hear.**

bl th wh

bl th wh

bl th wh

bl th wh

bl ch sh

bl ch sh

bl ch sh

bl ch sh

184

cry

crab

The consonant blend cr is used at the beginning of a word.
The cr makes the sound we hear at the beginning of crust.

1 Put a circle around the picture that starts with the sound cr.

crust   clock   crib   crate

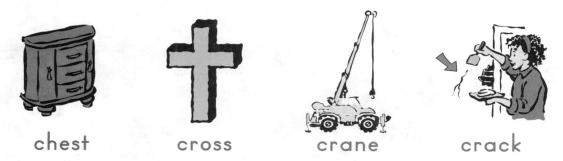

chest   cross   crane   crack

185

② **Practice printing** Cr **with a capital** C.

Cr

③ **Practice printing** cr **with lowercase letters.**

cr

④ **Circle the letters that make the beginning sound you hear.**

cl cr   cl cr   cl cr   cl cr

⑤ **Write the words in alphabetical order.**

a b c d e f g h i j k l m n o p q r s t u v w x y z

elephant   fish   clock   dog

1. _____   3. _____

2. _____   4. _____

186

6 Print the beginning consonant blends for each word below the picture.

| bl | br | cl | cr | wh | sh |

_____ eep

_____ oss

_____ istle

_____ and

_____ amp

_____ ack

7 Read the make-up words.

crade   cren   crif   croz   crub

8 **Look at the pictures. Choose the correct word from the word bank to complete the sentences. Print the words on the lines below.**

clam	crane	crawl

1. The _____ had a shell.

2. Blake can _____ .

3. The _____ was in the lake.

9 **Finish spelling the words under the pictures by filling in the beginning consonant blends.**

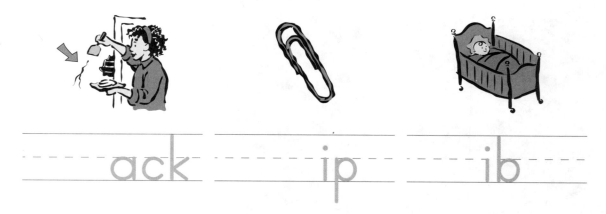

_____ ack   _____ ip   _____ ib

----

10 **Look at the pictures below. Print the beginning sound for each picture.**

11 **Draw a line from the puzzle phrase to the picture it matches.**

a crack
in the lake

a crane
with a crate

a crab
with a cramp

a dog
with a crutch

189

12 Write the sentences on the lines.

Mom will crush the crust.

Cram the crate with a crane.

The lad will crawl to cross the crag.

LESSON 40
Review: Blends cr, cl, br, bl

1 **Put a circle around each picture in the row that starts with the given sound.**

2 **Print the words from the word bank on each row that is marked with the beginning sound.**

brake	black	brad	blue
crate	clap	crop	clock

br _____ _____

bl _____ _____

cr _____ _____

cl _____ _____

3 **Draw a line from the picture to the word it matches.**

crutch

brake

crab

blade

clap

192

4 **Spell the words below the picture by printing the beginning sounds.**

amp   ate   ide

ack   ip   in

5 **Draw a line from the puzzle phrase to the picture it matches.**

a clam on
a clock

a branch on
a cross

a blimp on
a block

a brush on
a bridge

193

6 **Circle the words your teacher reads.**

brake	brave	blade

black	blade	blast

crate	crack	crib

clam	clock	clash

7 **Spell the words below the pictures by printing the ending sounds.**

fi   bru   ma

8 **Write the sentences below. Be sure to use a capital letter to begin the sentence and a question mark or period at the end of the sentence.**

What is your name?

_____

- -

My name is_____.

_____

- -

9 **Read the make-up words.**

clob   crob   blom   brom   clof

194